W9-BFS-853

Tsonakwa
and
Yolaikia

*Legends
in
Stone,
Bone, and
Wood*

Gamekeeper, Guardian of the Woodlands

Tsonakwa and Yolaikia

Legends in Stone, Bone, and Wood

Acknowledgements

We are grateful for assistance
and/or use of material from:

The Galleria, Norman, Oklahoma
Many Goats Gallery, Tucson, Arizona
The Raven Gallery, Minneapolis, Minnesota
Greentree Gallery, Philadelphia, Pennsylvania
Isis Productions
Norma Beale
Gary Crawford
Margo Ginsberg
Evelyn Harris
Kip Lilly and Jeannine Bayard
Raymond Shubinski

Credits

Editors: Linda Crawford, Jo West
Photographers: Linda Crawford, Jo West, Petronella Ytsma
Designer: Ruth Dean
Publisher: Arts and Learning Services Foundation
4632 Vincent Avenue South
Minneapolis, Minnesota 55410

© 1986 Arts and Learning Services Foundation
All rights reserved
ISBN 0-938541-03-X

Table of Contents

6   Preface

9   Introduction: In My Father's Hands

12   My Brother the Bear

14   The Creation

15   Sunset Elk

17   The Porcupine

18   Samoset

19   Caribou Man

21   Kuloscap and the Little Ghost

21   Kuloscap and the Whale

21   Kuloscap and Pujinkskwes

22   Kuloscap and the Ice Giants

23   Reflections

24   Chief of the Pond

27   The Buffalo Go

28   Deer Mother

29   The Cayuga Buffalo Dance

30   Shishigua

32   The Weeping Moon

33   Owl Mother and Child

34   Tsesuna Raven

37   Taiowa's Creation

38   Coyote and the Stars

39   Lintowaken

40   The Return

42   Walrus Story

45   Bear and Beaver

47   Great Bear

48   Tunghak Story

50   Quail Story

52   The Shaman

54   Yolaikia On Her Work

55   Land Mother/Water Mother

56   Father Sky/Mother Earth

57   Mother of the Mountain

58   Bird/Shaman Transformation Amulet

58   Owl Woman and Child Amulet

59   Bear Evolution

59   Abenaki Mother and Child

60   Red Deer Woman: Totem of the Wolves

60   First Deer

61   Wolf Clan Mother

62   Sky Woman

62   Shaman/Owl Transformation

Preface

Gerard Rancourt Tsonakwa and Yolai'kia Wapita'ska are artists, husband and wife, Abenaki Indians, and contemporary Americans. They bring all that they are to their work, so that each sculpture they create, each mask, and each story becomes a thread of light. It makes a visible connection between the legacy of Indian tradition and the world view of our present-day technocracy. Their art connects the tangible, everyday life around us with the unseen world of the spirit.

The role of the artist in society is to be the one who Sees. The art is his or her expression of that vision, and it is there for us, the viewers, to use to make visible the unseen. Tsonakwa, paraphrasing Sitting Bull, says, "My people have come a long way. And somewhere along that way we have lost something very precious to us. And now some of us must go back along the way we came and look very hard and carefully for those precious things we have lost."

The work of Tsonakwa and Yolaikia gently reminds us of the time in our history as a species when the strong psychic sense for what lies hidden in "the back of the cave" was a vital part of being alive. They speak of a time before we humans began pushing the environment so far away from ourselves that we "improved" life past the point of our needing to sense what we couldn't see. We let the psychic ability waste away, and now among the few depositories left are what Tsonakwa calls "the natural world societies—the Inuit, for example, and the Ainu, the Hottentot and the Gypsies, the American Indian tribes."

The masks and sculptures of Tsonakwa and Yolaikia depict the creatures of the world through their *inuas* or vital essences. They call forth the spirits of the unseen world, show the Mother of the Earth, the Wolf, the Bear, the Father of the Sky, the Sun and the Creation. The artists hollow out a space in the back of a mask or in stone as a resting place for the spirits. They put hoops around masks and sacred signs in carvings. They use healing stones from all four directions, pick-marked rocks from ancient Indian quarries, and crystals as pathways for the light that binds us to other worlds. The spirits who come to us are usually met with the surprise and even hostility that we tend to feel for aliens, but Tsonakwa says, "I have learned to welcome them into my dreams and in my work, to make a way for myself so that I will be welcome in theirs." Like the Dreamweaver, Tsonakwa and Yolaikia make tangible for us the beauty of the universe in the shapes and colors of art.

Yolaikia coaxes the natural shape of deer antler, a material traditionally sacred to women, into the creatures of this and other worlds—Father Sky and Mother Earth, and their offspring, Land Mother and Water Mother, and their descendants, Owl and Wolf and Deer and Woman. Her psychic world teems with life, and the forms are so full of energy that they seem in constant flux. The universe becomes a little unstuck, and the viewer is almost startled by a sense of the possibilities that exist for transformation. The world is the same and the world is new.

Tsonakwa the sculptor uses color like a painter. Refusing to be limited by the soapstone or alabaster or marble or wood he uses for the main body of his figures, he engraves and paints color into the surface, he inlays and bonds gemstones which he gathers from all over North America, until the finished piece sings with color. He creates his own dyes from the crushed rock left from the sculptures, mixes it with clay, and makes a ceramic-like finish for his wooden masks or totems that is natural-looking and exceedingly rich. There is a passion in his making that pushes him to the edge of what is technically possible, to make the right resting place for an ancient thought or a dream or an elusive presence.

In his storytelling Tsonakwa is a dreamweaver, too. Among the Abenaki, storytelling is a formal thing to a large degree, a way to remember history and maintain tradition. Tsonakwa uses it to unite us to our natural past, the "grandfather societies of earth." He tells stories about the people who are four-legged and winged and finned so that we may see ourselves sharing the sacred web of life with them. He tells new stories and old, Indian stories for all people, in the tradition of the personal contact that is created between people in the presence of the telling. Until now, he has been unwilling for the stories to be written down lest they lose their aliveness, for every time a story is retold, even though it may be word for word, it is something different, something new.

Think of these stories then, not as something closed, but as touch-stones, like the art itself, invitations to an exploration of the universe within and without. For as

Tsonakwa says, he will rise and pass from this place, and the stone and wood and words will be here far beyond him.

Linda Crawford

"What we do and say is what we leave to this world. It is to this care and keeping that I do my work, that people will know the name of my country that has been lost from the maps, the beautiful country, the Land of the Dawn, the land of the Abenaki."

Tsonakwa

Yolaikia

Introduction *In My Father's Hands*

When I went home to Sainte Methode, my village in Quebec, after twenty-three years, I found almost all my people gone, and those who were left were very old. I took some of the soil from where my house used to be and I ate it. I wanted it to be inside of me. My family had told me that the soil of that place is my flesh and the rocks are my bones and the waters my blood. That place is me. I left something there that was so special and delicate I was afraid to go back to see it.

All the time I have been away from my home I have thought of my family. When I was sixteen years old and my parents saw me off down the dusty road from Sainte Methode, I thought I would be back soon. Afterwards I often wondered what it would have been like if I had stayed home, what more I might have learned from my father and mother. For years my father urged me to come home and carve, and after his death, I began to carve again. Now when I make my masks and sculptures, my father and mother are with me. I have the overwhelming feeling of being a child again, of being close to that old source of love and security and guidance.

These art objects are my family now, for in the masks I see the faces of my beautiful aunts and uncles, my cousins, and parents, and grandparents. I think of the times we gathered together in the sugar bush, and often for the wood of the masks I use boards that I have taken from the old maple sugar house, our favorite gathering place. I think that the wood has kind of taken a picture of my family, and I can make that picture visible in the faces of the masks.

We told stories in that place, as an entertainment. We had no electricity, no radio, no television. Some people there still live with wood stoves and kerosene lamps, and it's not a bad life. If the weather is cold, they add more wood to the fire. We'd sit around it at night and tell stories. Everything was simple and personal.

In order to have my father and mother with me as much as I can now, I sit down and do the things that they taught me to do. Every time I carve a piece of stone or wood, my father sits next to me, just like when I was seven years old. He shows me how to use the tools, and he shows me what to make. And he reminds me of the important characteristics of each of my wild brothers and sisters of the forest as I carve them.

My father regarded things very simply. Sky is our father and Earth our mother who sustains all life. The flesh of Earth, the soil, we use to grow our food—the corn, the squash, and the beans. The stones are her bones. They are not dead at all, and anything that has life still retains that life when you use it. The things we make from stone have a spirit of their own. In the past, we used flints to make our arrow points and our knives and our tools. So I decided I would use flints for my tools now. I gather the flints in North Carolina in a place where people have gathered flint for 12,000 years to make fine tools. I feel good following the tradition—it's the oldest tradition I can think of in the world.

And from Pacolet, South Carolina, I gather pieces of soapstone from a quarry that Indians used to mine stone for pots 8000 years ago. I take the pieces left behind, and I can feel the hands of the ancient people upon those pieces still. I see my brothers and sisters in every piece of that stone—the bear, the beaver, the badger, the otter, the hawk, the owl, the eagle, and the salmon. All that I do is take the shapes that are there and I bring out the spirit. I only remove the stone that encases it, all the stone that isn't the thing that I want to see. And when I'm finished, I engrave the spirit lines and inlay them with gemstones from America. I use malachite and turquoise, pipestone and argillite, abalone and mother of pearl, azurite and agate—stones that have a special meaning, stones that are used for healing or to open up spiritual gateways to the other worlds.

It seems as though my people have always done these things. I cannot remember a time when there wasn't someone in our house either hunting or carving. It just was a natural thing for me to do. I never thought that someday I would show my work to people other than my family. I did the carving with reverence for the materials and the tools and the subject. We believe that there is a spirit in everything, whether the Creator made it or we did. The same spirit that moves a blade of grass moves me.

And today when I do my work, my spirit still goes into the things I make, through my hands or maybe through my heart. I know that my father's heart guides my hands, and if his heart doesn't guide me well, then my hands will be useless to him. And so I must always think about what I am doing. I must do

it in a spiritual manner or things won't come right for me. If I keep the doorway open in the top of my head, if I listen to the guidance of the people who have gone before me, then the work will be easy. It will go smoothly and nothing will break in my hands.

I think of my art as a monument to my people. I would rather make many small monuments, so that they do not break the contour of the land, but I see in each one of them the peaks and the valleys of my Laurentide mountains. I see the darkness and the light of the Mistassini Plateau. I see in them the shadows of great animals flickering through the foliage of our forests. Being an artist is the only way I can continue the culture of my family and my people. I am trying to do something fundamental so that it will last.

Many of my ideas have come to me in dreams. My father was a dreamer, and he taught himself to wake up from dreams and record very carefully the things he had seen. And he taught me to do the same. So most of what I do are the things of dreams. We have a belief that there is a being called a Dreamweaver who sits in the sky. He is the one who weaves the beauty of our lives like a great belt.

All the brightest colored beads he uses, and weaves a fine design. And when we begin our lives, we walk out in this belt and we are guided by its bright design all the days of our lives, until we reach the end.

If we live well, if we walk what we call the Good Red Road, we avoid *koyaanisqatsi*, the life out of balance. When I left my dear Quebec I came into a world I had only begun to understand in boarding schools in Canada. For a long time I had difficulty in dealing with different languages, different ways, different attitudes about life. I became trapped in the cities, accustomed to them in some ways, and in others I never blended in. I became a Métis, a walker between worlds, and I belonged to neither. I walked about and became sadder and sadder at what I saw—terrible treatment of my mother the Earth and a lack of regard for the spirit of things. I walked about with a life so small that I could carry it about under my fingernails.

After a long time, I felt that I had to choose one way of living or the other, and I chose the old way, the one I had known since the beginning of my memory, the one that made me happy. I took heart again in the old ways and did what my father had told me to do—carve monuments to my people, small monuments.

And then my life changed. A new spirit came back into me and my life became so great that the sky could not cover it, the mountains and forests of home could not contain it, and the wind and rivers could not move it. Now in every mask and every sculpture I hear a voice, like the wind blowing through the trees of the Mistassini. That great wind that blows out of the mountains and bends the boughs of the spruce and cedar whispers to every piece of stone and every piece of wood I carve. It says, "Look now, you too are an ancestor to generations still to be born." And though I make things of stone and wood, these things are not mine. The heart of my father guides me and I am in his hands.

Gerard Rancourt Tsonakwa

I know that the old ones lie sleeping in the great White Bear of my land. Their ways have not ended, but wait for springtime to fill the hearts of humankind. Then the ancient Bear will awaken and dance again, at last, on the earth.

Bear Cabinet

Ancient Bear Fetish

My Brother the Bear

The oldest song of my people's Wapiti, the wampum record of my people, says these things to me: *We are Abenaki. We follow the bear. There never was a time when we did not follow the bear, for the bear is our brother and we are Abenaki. It is from the bear that we learned our way of life, and he is the leader of all our clans, the chiefs, the warriors and the hunters. And it is from the bear that we learned to have confidence in our strength, and at the same time to be aware of our weaknesses. And it is from the bear we learned that true strength is very gentle, and power, great power, is seldom used.*

And so my father told me before he passed on the shining way, that once three Crees and their dog had hunted a full season in our Mistassini and Laurentide forests, and at the end of the season they were tired and in sore need of human companionship. They came to one of our villages where stayed Bedagi, my great-great-granduncle who was a great medicine man back in the days when our medicine was still powerful in the sacred web of life. And because our people saw that the Crees were tired and alone, they offered hospitality and took them in. A great feast there was of moose and deer and turkey and goose. And they sang the songs of the people long into the night, feasting and dancing. They told the stories of creation until all were tired, and then the three Crees and their dog were led to a small house at the edge of the village, there to find their sleep.

My father told me that those three Crees didn't go right to sleep. They lay awake thinking and still hungry, for though they had eaten the meat of the moose and the deer, the turkey and the goose, it is bear that the Cree really like to eat. For they are not brother to the bear, and bear meat is what they want. They were not satisfied.

And so in the darkest hours of the night, when the village was silent and all were asleep but the Crees, they crept out of that house and went off into the hills at the edge of the village. There they sought out the den where sleeps our brother the bear.

And the oldest Cree hunter took a lighted torch and went inside the den of the bear and aroused him from his sleep. They chased him out into the open; he was frightened, snarling, and growling. They chased him east and west, north and south. The bear's snarls and growls awakened Bedagi, and he was concerned about what was happening to our good brother the bear. He looked in time to see a Cree hunter shoot an arrow and wound our brother the bear so that he began to bleed. And the Cree dog, Bright Teeth, snapped at the bear so he could not find rest. Bedagi was afraid for the bear, so he made a powerful medicine, and it lifted the bear off the ground and the bear ran off into the sky. There he dripped blood down on the leaves of the maple and the sumac, and so these leaves turn red in my country in the fall even today.

So strong was the medicine that the three Crees and their dog, without knowing it, ran off the ground too, into the sky, chasing after the bear with their greed. Finally they looked down and saw the earth far below, and they shouted to one another, "Enough of this—we must go back! Look, we have left the earth behind!"

But Bedagi's medicine was too strong, and they could not return to Earth. So these Crees and their dog will chase our brother the bear through eternity in the sky, in the constellation known as the Great Bear. And though they are very hungry, they will never reach him until the last night of creation time. I know this story is true, because my father, Old Bear Grinning, told me.

Rainbow Bear

The Creation

A story told by Mary Bombadier,
Kiowa/Caddo

At first there was nothing. In the beginning there was nothing in all of time and space. Only was there darkness and Maheo. If Maheo was silent, then the Universe was silent. If Maheo was still, then the Universe was still and nothing could move. If Maheo listened, there was nothing to hear. When he looked, there was nothing to see. All around Maheo was nothingness and silence, age upon age.

Maheo was great and powerful—his being was the Universe. He was not lonesome because he was everything. Maheo thought to himself, "With the power I have and with all my being, I could make something. Power is nothing until it has been used to do something." As he moved through endless nothingness, Maheo thought to himself, "I shall make the Universe."

With his great power and knowledge, Maheo decided what to do. He took all of time, past and present and future, and gathered it in one hand. Into his other hand he gathered all space. With these in each hand he clapped. A great clap it was, greater than thunder, for this clap was the first sound ever heard in the Universe.

Out of Maheo's hands then came all things, and everything from which all things could be made. Stars came flying out of his hands like sparks from crackling wood in a fire. Everywhere did the stars fly out, and they continue to fly out and burn today everywhere across the night-time sky. This is how time began and all things began to be made.

Abenaki Dawn

Sunset Elk

The bull elk stands, antlers high in
the sun of autumn.
His powers will be tried in the
rutting against other strong ones.
The does wait.

One autumn, the old elk will be too weary
His eyes dim, his legs feeble,
He will lay himself down
And the young bucks will come,
Touch antlers to his,
In memory.

Sunset Elk

Great Porcupine

The Porcupine

When I was young we didn't have any pets in my home. We had dogs that were for hunting, but we had no time or resources for pets. And so in the evening I would go out into the forest behind our house and meet with some friends there in a clearing. My favorites were the porcupines. They came out in the evening to eat the little trees, and they're not much afraid of humans. Because they have such good protection from their quills, they imagine they can handle anything in the world, and they don't have to run away. So I could come close to them. I'd go out into the forest and I'd bring them food—things like carrots and sweet things to eat, things they like very much. And they'd go home and say, "Hey, the man gave us something good to eat—that boy over there." And I'd go into my house and I wouldn't say anything. I had a pet, a friend.

Whenever my grandmother or my mother or my aunt needed some quills from the porcupine, I'd go with a piece of apple and a carrot and a blanket. I'd give the porcupine the apple and the carrot and make him happy. Then I'd throw the blanket over him and shake it around a little. And I'd take the blanket off and the porcupine wondered, "Now, what's the matter with him?" And I got his quills in the blanket. And he went home and had the carrot and the apple, and I'd go home and I'd get ten cents, and it was all mine. I had a very good feeling about the porcupine. I loved him.

I left him and went away and I didn't think about my friend the porcupine for a long, long time. One day, in the bloody mud of Viet Nam, my old friend the porcupine came back to my mind. I thought, "Well, that porcupine has been gone a long time. All that's left of him now are his grandchildren. And I wonder if my friend ever told his grandchildren about me. If I went home, would they know about me? Would my name still be in that place? And I thought about my friend the porcupine. We were good neighbors although we never spoke. I didn't know Porcupine and he didn't know Abenaki. But he got what he needed from me and I got what I needed from him. And now I see this world filled with people who could speak, but they don't. Or they shout, and they don't try to listen or understand. And I wonder how this can be, considering that the porcupine and I could understand each other without a word. We were good neighbors, and I still remember him, five generations later for porcupines.

Samoset

Samoset was an Abenaki warrior and chief who lived in New England in the early 1600's. It is said that he was the first Indian to make friends with the English settlers at Plymouth. It was Samoset and his people who introduced the settlers to the land and the ways to survive upon it. He sat with them at the first harvest feast, and he invited the English to join with him in a dance of prayer and thanksgiving. Afterwards, he was accused of witchcraft. Some say he was shipped to England where he died in prison at Portsmouth in 1637. Others say he was burned at the stake.

Samoset

Caribou Man

Caribou Man was a lifelong friend of my father, who first saw him in a dream when he was six or seven years old. My father was walking down a forest path when Caribou Man loomed up out of the ground in front of him. Caribou Man was so surprised to see my father that he ran away, and that was all there was to that first dream. My father learned that in the dream world we are intruders. We are apparitions, and we can be very frightening to the spirits there. When my father saw Caribou Man for the second time, he was about eleven years old. He approached him calmly so Caribou Man would not be scared. They stared at each other, and they came to know one another.

My father dreamed of Caribou Man seven times in his life. They came to be good friends, and Caribou Man told him things that would happen in the future. Sometimes my father made carvings of Caribou Man's face, and then he would remember things Caribou Man had told him. In his dreams they might have seemed meaningless, but suddenly the meaning would become clear. Now that my father has passed on to the other side, I'm sure he sees a lot of Caribou Man. Now I carve Caribou Man's face in hopes that I will see him one day. If I approach him calmly, so as not to frighten him away, maybe he will stop to tell me how my father is doing.

Caribou Man

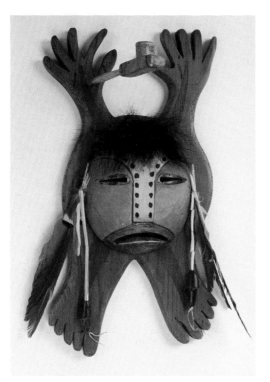

Little Ghost

Kuloscap

Kuloscap and the Little Ghost

Kuloscap is a true person who lived long ago, before there was a written language among my people, and many of our legends are about him. When I was little my father used to tell a story about Kuloscap and the ghosts. One time a whole bunch of ghosts came before Kuloscap to scare him. There were big ghosts and little ghosts, red ghosts, white ghosts, black ghosts, horrible ghosts and ugly ghosts. They all tried to frighten Kuloscap, but he treated them with disdain, except one tiny ghost who was very awkward, not sure of himself, and not scarey at all. Kuloscap took pity on this little ghost who was trying so hard, and although all the ghosts together couldn't scare the great Kuloscap, he made believe he was afraid of the little ghost. When the little ghost saw Kuloscap's fear, he gained courage, and he took advantage of Kuloscap's nature. He said to himself, "If he's so afraid of me, I'll take his pipe." And the little ghost took Kuloscap's pipe and ran off with it, believing that he was so frightening that Kuloscap would do nothing. Now, Kuloscap's pipe was his favorite thing. Kuloscap wondered about his decision, wondered if it had been such a good idea after all—to make a big ghost out of such a little one. Ever after, my people have gathered together to make decisions. They keep silence for 24 hours, then consider how the decision will affect people seven generations later, so that they will not regret what they have done.

Kuloscap and the Whale

Kuloscap even taught the whales to smoke. When he crossed the Mackinac Straits one time, he bribed a whale with a gift of tobacco to give him a ride on his back. And the whale got Kuloscap halfway out across the straits and said, "Kuloscap, now that I have you in the middle of the water, I will set my price. What I want is your great pipe, so that I can smoke. And you must show me how to smoke it before I will take you to the other side." And so it was. Kuloscap gave his great pipe to the whale and taught him how to smoke it. And any time you see whales, you can see them blowing "smoke" in the air. This is how they learned to smoke their pipes.

Kuloscap and Pujinkskwes

There have always been pujinkskwes, witches, that have lived among our people. Once a pujinkskwes came to Kuloscap where he sat on his favorite hill with his beautiful pipe. It was a great big pipe, enough pipe so that fifteen men could smoke it. Kuloscap always loved his pipe.

Pujinkskwes said to him, "I have a great pipe too. If my pipe is greater than yours, then you must leave this land and I will take control." Kuloscap laughed and said, "You cannot possibly have a pipe better than mine, for mine is a great pipe, and it's enough pipe for fifteen men to smoke." Pujinkskwes said, "Here, see my pipe." And she put a pound of tobacco in her pipe, so great it was. When she lit it up it was so powerful that the tree Kuloscap sat next to cracked open—that's how powerful was that pipe! Old Kuloscap laughed and said, "Ha, my pipe is better than that." And he loaded his pipe with *five* pounds of tobacco and smoked it. And so great was his pipe that the earth cracked, and it swallowed Pujinkskwes, and she didn't laugh anymore.

Kuloscap and the Ice Giants

The great Abenaki hero Kuloscap battled the ice giants. The ice giants had gotten too strong and were blowing their cold breath so that winter was long and harsh, and the other seasons were so short they almost disappeared. Kuloscap met with some of his friends, and it was decided that he should go North to the back door of the world, fight with the ice giants, and slam the door shut on them. This he did. And Kuloscap decided to take from each ice giant his great stone bracelet so he could prove on his return that he had accomplished his task. As he defeated the ice giants, one by one, and gathered their stone bracelets, his task became more and more burdensome. Finally, after killing many, he said, "Enough of this! I'm getting tired with these heavy things! It's harder carrying these bracelets than killing ice giants!" By that time he had killed 27 ice giants, and had a bracelet for each of the great *sachems* of the Abenaki. He returned home, leaving some of the ice giants alive, and that is why we still have winter today.

When Kuloscap returned with the bracelets to the Abenaki, he fashioned each one into a stone box to hold the Wapitis, the covenants of the League of the Wabenaki.

Crystal Box—Ice Giant's Bracelet

22

Reflections

I come from a water world, and in those lakes and rivers everything was doubled. I saw the moose and the moose underneath, the tree and the tree underneath, the rainbows and the sunrise and the sunset, all above and below. It was as if I saw the physical being and then the spiritual being underneath, supporting it. There is the bear, and there is his double, the spirit of the bear. Technology tends to separate us from our shadows.

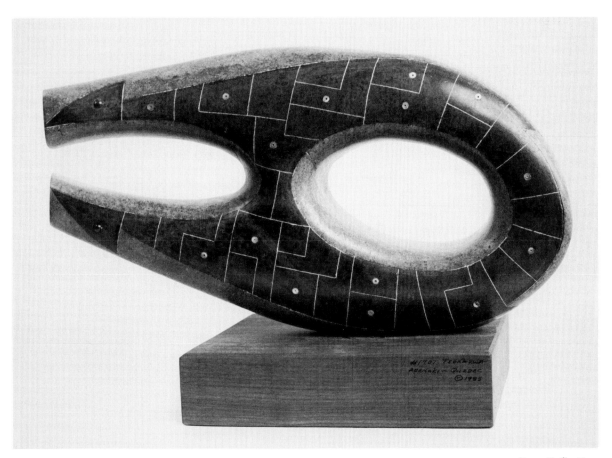

Bear Reflection

Chief of the Pond

There was a pond with many beautiful creatures—frogs, fish, snakes—and the chief of the pond was a log. The log just lay in the pond every day, and all the creatures did as they pleased. The log just lay there and was the chief, and that's all. And then one day, a great and beautiful bird landed at the edge of the pond, a white wading bird with long legs and a long beak. He was beautiful and elegant, graceful in his colors and in the way that he moved about. And all the creatures in the pond saw this beautiful bird that had come from they didn't know where, and they admired him very much. They spoke to one another saying, "This one is beautiful. Look at him. He could lead us to greatness. He could make our pond great if he were our chief. For look at our chief! He is a log, and he sleeps all day and does nothing. But this bird—he moves about elegantly and he is beautiful. Great things he could lead us to." And the animals got together and held a council, and they decided to make this great bird the chief. And within a week or two there was no one left in the pond except the bird chief. For the chief was a heron, and herons love to eat frogs and fish and snakes. And that's the story of the chief log and the chief bird.

Jewel Fish is the spirit of all fish. He flows through his waterworld as water and light flow through him.

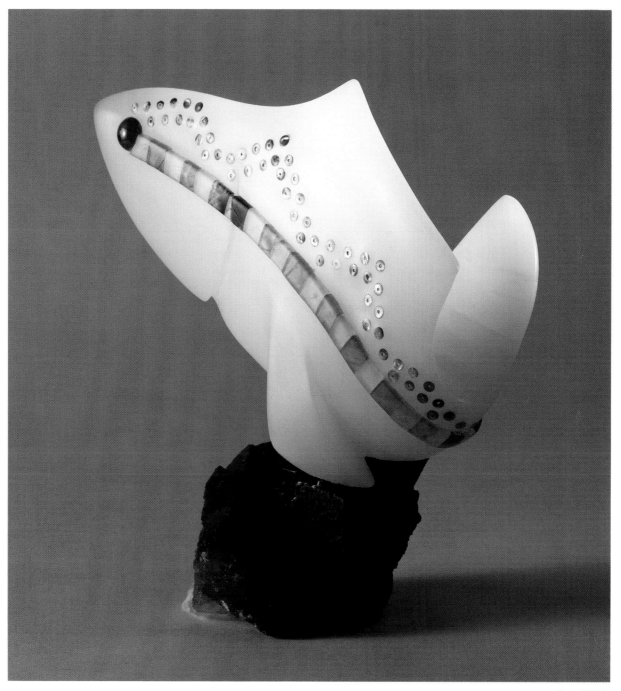

Jewel Fish

Buffalo Mother and Child

The Buffalo Go

A Kiowa/Comanche Legend told by
Old Lady Horse (Kiowa)

It is estimated that in 1850 sixty million buffalo roamed the plains of the United States and Canada— twice as many buffalo as people in North America. By 1902 there were less than 1,000 buffalo left, and many of them were confined to zoos. As the buffalo disappeared, the Kiowa and Comanche people could foresee the end of their world, the end of their buffalo-hunting life.

Everything the people had came from the buffalo. They ate the meat of the buffalo and little else. Their lodges were made from buffalo skins, as were their clothing and sleeping mats. From the bones of the buffalo they made knives and spears. The horns were sacred, used for bonnets and rattles. The buffalo were part of the religion of the people, for each animal had within it a Manitou, or spirit. When a buffalo was killed, offerings and prayers were made right away, so that the Manitou would turn back into a living buffalo. In that way the buffalo would never die.

When the railroads and ranches started cutting across buffalo range, war came to the Plains.

One day, one of the last free bands of the Kiowa was camped on the south side of Mount Scott in Oklahoma. A woman got up very early that morning to draw water from Medicine Creek. She looked into the red clouds of sunrise, and there she saw the last buffalo herd, a ghost herd, walking slowly through the clouded sky. Right to Mount Scott they walked, that spirit herd. A great bull was in the lead, a spirit bull, and several cows and calves followed.

Just as a storm began to break, great thunder rolled, and Mount Scott opened up a huge crack. The buffalo spirit herd walked right in. Inside was a place of great beauty, a springtime place with cotton-woods in bloom and the smell of new grass. When the spirit herd walked inside, the mountain closed behind them.

The woman ran back to awaken her people and tell them the vision she had seen there in the dawn. When the elders heard her story, great sadness came to them. They knew that the buffalo were beaten and were gone forever from the plains.

That night as the stars blinked over Mount Scott while the Kiowa people were dancing, the great buffalo leader appeared in the stars. He stands there still, in the constellation some people call Pegasus, as the answer to Kiowa prayers. He stands there to give hope to Indian people.

Deer Mother

Deer Mother

At the beginning of the world, my people were wasting away because they had nothing to eat. Pujinkskwes dug a hole in the earth, the origin of all life, and out of that hole she brought deer. She brought them out all day. There were so many deer we called them mosquitoes! And my people took the life of the deer, but we did not take the spirit.

I was told that the earth feeds the grass and the grass feeds the deer and the deer feeds humans. I would ask, "What is it that humans feed?" I was told that we are the ones who walk and think, and that's the difference. We have the heart that feels and the mind that thinks, and if we put those together with our voice, we can pray. In the prayers of my people are prayers for grass, for the renewal of the earth, and for deer. And if we do this thing, if we pray, then all of this life and all of this spirit will go on forever.

The Cayuga Buffalo Dance

The good hunter whose heart is true always seeks to make his peace with the spirit of the buffalo whom he hunts. He must take only that which he needs to sustain his physical life. He pays homage to the buffalo spirit and does not take that. In this way he knows there will always be buffalo. The Buffalo Dance is performed before the hunt so that the buffalo spirit may be appeased. Buffalo is asked to share some of his life with the hunter, and in return, the hunter promises that Buffalo will be exalted, and the continuation of his kind assured. The original Buffalo Dance, which began with the Kiowa in the Southern Plains in the mid-1700's, moved north and east and spread among many tribes. The Kiowa used a mask that was made from the skin of the head of the buffalo. As the dance moved farther and farther from its origin, the masks changed, and were made with materials familiar to the various mask-makers. By the late 1800's the Kiowa Buffalo Dance had found its way to the Northeastern Woodlands and had become very popular among the Cayuga. It seems strange that people who never knew or hunted the buffalo came to do the Buffalo Dance.

Cayuga Buffalo Dance Mask

Shishigua

It was long ago, when this whole world was new. The Great Father finished making the mountains and the valleys and he put the waters where they all should be. Then he decided to fill this world with creatures of every kind. For each one he made a body of clay. With his own breath he filled them with life. Each one he would touch upon the head so they could think and learn, upon the heart so they could feel love. And so it was that the Great Father decided that he would make a beautiful lizard that he would call Shishigua—Snake. So the Great Father took clay and he rolled it out into a long strip like those we use to make a coiled pot. This was the body of Shishigua. But when the Great Father reached in his pot for more clay to make Shishigua's legs, the pot was empty.

And so the Great Father said to Shishigua, "Snake, you must wait here, and I must go to the river and gather more clay to make your legs." And so it was. The Great Father went to the river to gather clay and Shishigua waited. He waited for a long time, and finally he said to himself, "I don't wish to wait here any longer. I wish to go out and see the great beauty of this creation world for myself. And so it

was. With no legs, Shishigua crawled off into the grass and he was gone. Then the Great Father returned and he worried in his heart, saying to himself, "Poor Shishigua. He is gone and I didn't get to finish him. He doesn't have any legs. But worse than that, he doesn't have any skin. How will he live?"

And so it was. Shishigua was off in the grass with no legs and no skin. He saw the great beauty of this creation world and he loved it, but time passed, and the sun went down, and that night was very cold. Shishigua didn't have any skin to keep him warm, and pretty soon he started to freeze. He crawled into a wigwam to warm up alongside a woman's fire, but she was frightened of him and she screamed, and Shishigua crawled off again into the cold. He crawled into another wigwam to warm up by a man's fire, but the man hit him with a stick and hurt him. Shishigua crawled outside again, and he looked for a place on the ground to lay himself down to die.

Poor Snake, he didn't understand. But as he crawled along the ground, he saw something lying there, a fine beaded belt. Shishigua thought about making a skin from

this beautiful beaded belt: "These fine colors would keep me warm and I would not die. I would be beautiful and Woman wouldn't scream at me, and Man wouldn't hit me with a stick."

So right where those beads were lying on the ground, Shishigua crawled up on them and the beads began to stick to his skinless body. He rolled over and over on the beads, and more and more beads stuck, and soon Shishigua was all covered with bright shiny beads, from his nose to his tail.

This is how Shishigua, the grandfather of snakes, got his fine beaded skin, that first evening of creation time so long ago.

Shishigua

Weeping Moon

The Weeping Moon

The Moon is the sister of our mother the Earth. Always she watches her sister, and Earth responds with the ebb and flow of her waters. Moon has been watching a long, long time—so long that she has seen all the changes that Earth has endured. These make her sad. Where once animals and people lived together in harmony in a beautiful green world, now the people have driven the animals out and built structures where they hide from each other. Where once Earth's waters ran clear, now they are tainted. Where once the air was pristine and Moon could easily admire the beauty of her sister, her view is dimmed by dirt in Earth's breathing layer. And now Moon sees that man has taken to the sky, has visited her personally, and left trash behind! She weeps for her sister Earth and for herself.

Owl Mother and Child

The Owl Woman is a nighttime,
moon time, medicine entity.
Among my people, all females born
at night will have spiritual gifts,
whereas those born in the day will
excel in the social and political.
The newborn is cleansed by an
aunt and then given to her grand-
mothers, who charge her with
being human in the Abenaki
welcoming song:
Welcome to my world
I have been here a long time
I have heard it whispered in the breezes
of the forest
I have heard it whispered in the grasses,
bushes, and trees
Look now, little child,
Already you are an ancestor to generations
Yet to be born.

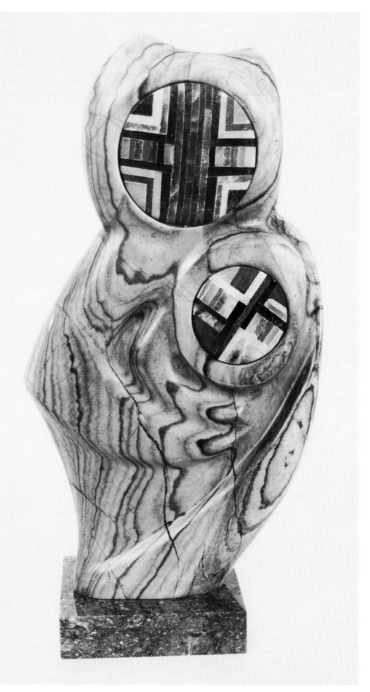

Owl Mother and Child

Tsesuna Raven

Tsesuna Raven Mask

It was long ago in the beginning of the world, and already there was evil planted upon the earth. Raven in those days was called Tsesuna, and he was the son of Thunderbird. Thunderbird's fate in life was to go about the earth destroying evil. Tsesuna was engaged in the same kind of task, except that his job was to seek out good. At that time, in the beginning of the creation world, Tsesuna was not the way you see him now. He was the most beautiful of all creatures, with a fine, bright rainbow of color in his wings, and a song, the sweetest, saddest of all.

One day Tsesuna was flying over the Laurentide Forest of my home, and there in a clearing in the forest he saw a beautiful great Longhouse of my people. He landed upon the earth, right outside the east door of the Longhouse, and he peered inside the darkness there. At the back of the house he saw a bright and cheerful fire. And so he stepped inside the house. But when he did, the house came to life, for a great living being it was, and it began to breathe. And the house spoke to Tsesuna saying these wonderful things: "And now, Tsesuna, you sit by my fire, and this is no common fire indeed, for this is the fire of life. The warmth of this fire is love, and it warms the hearts of people against the cold winds of loneliness and hate, so that the spirit will not sicken and die, and the race will always survive. And the light of this fire is the light of wisdom that comes with learning as we walk through the seasons on life's way. And Tsesuna, you take this fire of life and plant it in the hearts and minds of humankind, and let it warm and light the world."

And then the fire flared up bright and hot. But brave Tsesuna stepped right inside, searing and burning his feathers. He took a stick from the very center of the flame, and this he brought to humankind. But as he carried the burning branch, the heat of it seared away his voice. For us did Raven give up his glorious color and his lovely voice, so that we might have the fire of life, the light that sits somewhere behind our eyes, and the warmth in the core of our being that we call love. And thus to this day is the great Longhouse of the Abenaki called The House that Raven Found.

Tsesuna Raven

Sun Shower

Taiowa's Creation

A story told by Tawak Waptua, Bear Clan, Hopi

Taiowa moved endlessly through the Universe. His work of creation was to begin. His nephew, Soktuknang, he called across the heavens and said, "Now we shall make the world and it shall be filled with life. You shall make the earth to be the mother of all life. I will shine upon the earth and take away the darkness. I will be the light and father of all life.

So it was that the world was made by Soktuknang out of the Topela, endless space. He gathered everything into solid substance, some earth, some water. Then Soktuknang went to Taiowa and said, "I want you to see what I have done and if I have done well." "It is very good," said Taiowa, "but you are not done with it. Now you must create life in all kinds, and set it in motion according to my plan."

Then Soktuknang went into space and gathered substance to create his helper, Koyangworti, Spider Woman. "Look all about you, Spider Woman," said Soktuknang, "Here now is endless space and the world. But in the world there is no joyful movement. You should make all life, and at the end of your work, humankind and the world will be prepared for Taiowa's coming."

Spider Woman began. Taking substances from the earth, she began with the bearers of seeds, nuts, and fruits, to clothe the earth. Then she made four-legged creatures, creatures with wings, creatures with fur, and set them before her and behind her, to the right and to the left, and said, "Now go to the four corners of the world, go out in the four directions and fill this world with beauty, the joyful movement of life." And so it was done that the world was prepared with life. Taiowa looked now at the world all filled with life and said, "It is good. Now it is time to complete the plan."

In the darkness, Soktuknang stood in the sky to be the pattern by which Spider Woman would create humankind. In that darkness before the dawn of creation, Spider Woman gathered clay from each of the four directions, red, white, black, and yellow, and began molding from each clay a man and a woman in the shape of Soktuknang. While she worked, Spider Woman sang the creation song. These four men and four women, the four races, she made, and covered them with her white cape. Then, at the time of the dark purple light of dawn that first morning of creation, Spider Woman lifted her cape and the bodies of the people were solidified.

At the time of the yellow light of dawn, the humans awakened, but there was still dampness in the clay of their heads, and a soft spot there. It was through here that the breath of life entered them. Soon the sun appeared above the horizon, drying the remaining dampness in their bodies, and warming the people with love and knowledge. The people arose, a man and a woman of each of the four sacred colors, red, white, black, and yellow. Finished and solid, they stood and proudly faced the sun. "That is your creator," said Spider Woman. "The sun is your father and the creator of all things. You shall love him. You stand upon the Earth, who is your mother, the sustainer of all life. You shall love her." It was finished that way.

Coyote and the Stars

On the second morning of creation time, the Great Father set about the great task of filling the nighttime sky with beauty. He took a bag and he went out on the muskeg, and there he picked the little flowers we call Morning Stars. He filled the bag with the star flowers, and then he cut a long stick so that he could put the flowers on the end of the stick and place them in the sky just so, in a fine pattern, like beadwork. Then he found the highest hill in the land, so that from that high place he could set the little flowers in the sky, just so. But when he had climbed the mountain it was still light, so the Great Father decided to take a nap.

So he laid the bag down in the shade of a tree. And while he was sleeping, Coyote came along. Coyote is like all dogs—he's always thinking of food. He saw the Creator sleeping, and right nearby a great bag filled with something. Coyote said to himself, "I bet there's food in that bag. I'm going to look inside and see." So Coyote grabbed the bag and ran off. But as he ran, he tripped and fell, and the bag ripped open and the stars spilled out and flashed across the sky, every which-way. Then the Great Creator woke up from his nap, and the first thing he saw

were his stars flashing all across the sky. And he looked down, and he saw Coyote standing there with the bag in his teeth, ripped open. And the Great Father said to Coyote, "Look what you've done! I wished to put those stars in the sky in a fine pattern, like beads, and look at the mess you've made!"

Poor Coyote. He looked up and tears filled his eyes as shame filled his heart to see what he had done to the night sky. And Coyote began to howl. This is why today the stars are scattered all across the sky every which-way, and this is why coyotes, when they see the night sky and the mess their great-grandfather made, fill up with shame and howl.

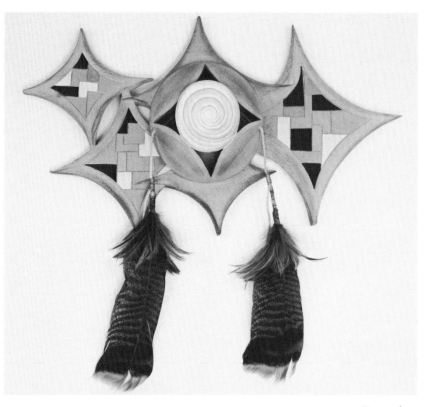

Starmaker

38

Lintowaken

an Abenaki song, c. 1690

A ni quwenotin U!
Beski qit-el-apin elmi-nelemwik elmi-papkiyik;
beski qit-el-apin.
Ani quwenotin U!

Neket-lo he-eli-alnisukmekwepen sipayi kuspemik,
etutch welinakwesitpen wutcowuk; he-eli-
match-pik lamiskin mipisul.
A ni quwenotin U!

Oh, it is long!
Lonely thou look upstream and downstream too;
Lonely thou look.
Oh, it is long!

Once as I went out in a canoe on the lake,
How beautiful were the mountains,
How green the leaves came out
Oh, it is long!

How fair the moon! We were very joyful.
Until I die, I will think of you.
Oh, it is long!

Then once more we shall go in a canoe when
I return to you;
When in the lonely winter wood here on the
mountain you wait;
Oh it is long!

Lonely thou look upstream and downstream too;
Lonely thou look.
Oh it is long!

Lonely thou look upstream
In spring and autumn;
Perhaps you might see me looking for you.
Oh it is long!

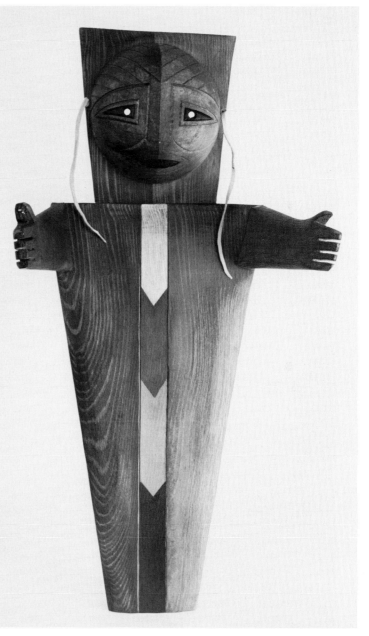

Housepost Manitou

The Return

There was a young man who lived in my town a long time ago. He lived there back when my people walked on the Good Red Road. They knew that the Earth was their mother and the Sky was their father. There was great joy in our village. It was a living thing, that place, and everyone knew it. The people got along and shared with each other. Doors were open. There was peace in that place.

One day the young man went off to hunt with the Cree for a short time. But years flew by, and when he finally returned he was a much older man. Times had changed; life had changed in the town. People no longer walked on the Good Red Road. Where there had been sharing, there was now selfishness and jealousy. And where people used to give, now they stole from one another. Where there had been love, there was hate. They closed their doors at night and locked them. There was no peace in that place.

And when that man saw these terrible things, something happened to him. He walked around with his head bowed and his shoulders bent. He went about crying out in a high, sad voice, "My people, what has come to you in this place of peace? Why have you walked off the Good Red Road? Where is the life we once knew? My people, we must learn love and peace again."

And his words echoed off the Laurentide Mountains and were swallowed in the mists of the Saguenay River. No one heard him. Day after day he shouted his message of peace and love, and the people pushed him aside. He was in the way. The children taunted him, "Quiet, old man!"

Year after year that man shouted his message of peace and love to the world. Time passed, and he was a very old, old man crying out, "My people, we must learn to love again. There must be peace in the world!"

Finally one day, a young man came up to the old man, the first person to really speak to him in twenty years or more. And the young man said, "Old man, since I was a child in my mother's arms, I have heard you going through our village shouting this foolish message of peace and love to the world. You break your heart every day with it. Can't you see that nothing has changed? The people still lie and cheat and steal and hate, and for all your shouting and all your tears, you have accomplished nothing. Why don't you stop this nonsense and rest yourself now? Can't you see, this world will not change—you cannot change it."

The old man looked at the young man, and deep sadness came into his eyes. He shook his head, and he said, "Yes, I see what you are saying, young man. It is true. I have shouted my message of peace and love for a long time, and I can see it is as you say—nothing has changed. And so it must be true, as you say, I cannot change this world. But one thing I want you to know, young man, before you pass me today, one thing I wish for you to understand—I do not shout my message to change this world. I shout my message so that this world will not change me."

Family Pictograph

Walrus Story

There is no word in Abenaki that means "animal." We think of all creatures as people—the people with fins and four legs, the people with wings and no legs. This is a story about people with flippers.

Once a group of Inuit (Eskimo) hunters crept up on some walruses and threw their harpoons. As the Inuit approached from the land side, all the walruses fled into the water. They swam far out into the sea, except, of course, for the one that had been harpooned. He was caught with the line and he could swim only a little way. He called out, and his mate looked back and swam to him. She locked her tusks with his and pulled him hard, but she could not break the line. Finally she swam a little way off, and for a long time wailed, mourning the loss of her mate.

I won't forget that old couple, their eyes as old as trilobytes, eternally locked in faces of stone, staring out in mild surprise at a world with changes greater than walruses have known. My Walrus Spirit Mask invites the *inua* of walrus to dwell in the hollow place in the back, that its spirit may feel welcome in this world.

Walrus Spirit

Crystal Beaver

Bear and Beaver

The crystals are the whispered directions to Beaver from the Creator.

In the beginning of the creation world, when Bear and Beaver were comrades and spoke the same language, Bear spent most of his time looking for sweet things to eat, especially the honey of the bees. He raided so many hives, in fact, that the bees held a great council and decided to move their hives to the tops of the trees, where they could not be reached by Bear.

After falling out of trees many times in unsuccessful attempts to reach the honey, Bear sat with his friend Beaver and lamented that he might never taste the sweetness of honey again. As Beaver tried to console him, Bear looked at his friend and saw him in a new light. He noted, as Beaver spoke soothingly to him, Beaver's large, sharp front teeth. Bear started to think, and his thoughts were not good ones. He said to Beaver, "With those teeth you could cut down a tree for me, and then the honey would be within easy reach!" But Beaver was afraid to accommodate his friend. He knew that trees deserve their lives, and bees are entitled to their honey.

Bear was persistent, though, and after much nagging Beaver finally gave in. He agreed to cut down one tree. But the honey from the top of that tree wasn't enough for Bear. There was more pleading, and more trees fell, until the Creator himself noticed that his forest was thinning. He caught Beaver in the act of cutting down a tree. Bear was standing some distance away, where the top of the tree would land, so the Creator didn't notice him. The Creator called down with a mighty voice to Beaver and demanded an explanation. Beaver stared in surprise. Bear hid in the bushes, shivering with fear. And because Beaver didn't want to get his friend in trouble, he lied, and said his teeth itched, and that chewing wood made them feel better.

The Creator knew Beaver was lying, and he gave a punishment to Beaver that he and all beavers would do hard work cutting trees, dragging them this way and that and piling them this way and that for all of time. Now, whenever Bear and Beaver meet at the water's edge, they only look at each other; they never speak.

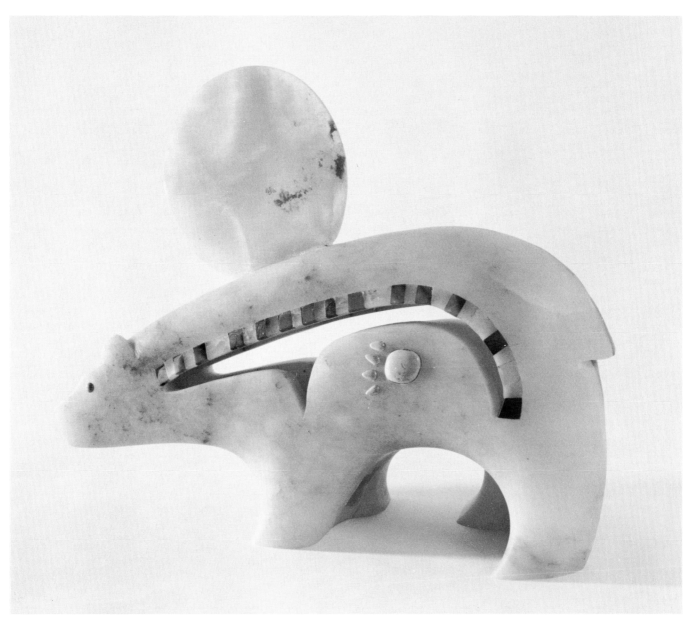

Northern Lights and Midnight Sun

Great Bear

The name of my land is Aben, the Land of the Dawn. In that land sleeps the Great Bear, the ancient league of my people. Lifeless in the sleep of hibernation, the Great Bear waits for spring.

When winter comes to Aben, the rivers freeze, and we see no fish. The maples stand leafless and stiff. The animals dig holes in the earth to hide safely inside our mother. And the geese fly south—a great mystery. Sickness comes in the winter, and the infirm ones die. And it is at this time of year that the Northern Lights hang like curtains in the sky. They are reflected in ice and on crusted snow. A great and mournful sound there is, so deep and final that I am fearful. Finally the sun rises again, and my dread, like the snow, melts away. With the return of Spring, the rivers melt and are filled with the splashing of fish. The animals come dancing out of the earth, the birds crying in the broken sky, and the hills turn a green we have never seen before.

I know that the old ones, and all of life that has gone before, lie sleeping in the Great White Bear of my land. Their time and ways have not ended, but only wait for springtime to fill the hearts of humankind. In that springtime will come the smell of new grass. The rivers will run clear and sweet, and the sun will feel so warm on our skins that the ancient Bear will awaken and dance again, at last, on the earth.

Torngat

Tunghak Story

An Ungavamiut (Eskimo) man who was very sick was brought by his family to a Naskapi-Ungavamiut shaman. The shaman diagnosed winter hysteria and treated the patient. The Ungavamiut went home cured, and a short time later the shaman became ill and killed himself. He had misjudged the strength of the powerful anti-life force of the *tunghak* that had inhabited the Ungavamiut. The shaman had drawn out the illness, and the *tunghak* that caused the illness, from his patient, and had taken them inside himself. There, in his familiar interior battleground, where he had successfully wrestled with diseases time after time, he was finally overcome by a *tunghak* force that was greater than his own.

Tunghak is the opposite of everything we know as life and love and warmth. *Tunghak* takes the wood out of life so there is nothing to burn. It takes away the motor force, so there is no movement. *Tunghak* is the tension in our daily lives. That doesn't mean that it is "bad" and that its opposite, *inua*, the life force given to us at birth, is "good." Like humans, the *tunghak* simply has its own nature of being.

Shaman Bringing Forth

Quail Story

Long ago when the world was new, our Great Father made all creatures, and gave them a way and a place to live. But some of the animals didn't like what they were given. Some became envious of others. Snapping Turtle tried living in the desert, but it didn't work. Salmon wanted to fly like a bird, and he still leaps today. But the most amazing of all were the quails. They so admired the elk that they wanted to be the elk. So they had a meeting where they squabbled about how they could be more elk-like.

One of the young quails took leaves from a blueberry bush, stuck them on top of his head, and strutted around puffing out his chest and admiring himself, saying, "Now, these look like the great antlers of the elk! I should be the leader of our herd!" At the next meeting, all the other quail, wanting to be like their self-proclaimed leader, ran off to the blueberry brambles to gather their own antlers. They were all so impressed with their new look that they exclaimed, "Now we are all elk!"

So it is today that quail sport fancy little "antler" feathers and prefer walking to flying. They move this way and that in herds along the ground, trying to graze and migrate like the elk. And there is always one quail who stands apart on higher ground watching out for the herd, like the great bull elk. But mostly, you hear quail in the brush at their little meetings, squabbling about who has the greatest "antlers" of all.

Quail

The Shaman

The shaman is full of *inua*, the fire of life. It is present in him in the form of wisdom and warmth. He gives great regard to the spiritual, and passes between the physical and the unseen worlds by means of song and dance and ritual transformation. He becomes one of those fine, tenuous strands supporting the sacred web of life. He is being in motion, always travelling between worlds carrying information. With his superior physical and psychic powers, he cures the sick, empowers the community to act on its own behalf, and brings forth the balance of the spiritual to the physical life of the people. With the help of the shaman, we can walk more gently within the sacred web of life.

Shaman in Flight

Yolaikia on her work

From the antlers of the deer and elk and moose, I carve the animals and spirits I know. Antler, like bone and horn, represents the seed of new life. Shed seasonally by the deer, it suggests the regenerative powers on earth. Among my people, antler and buffalo horn were used almost exclusively by women healers, many of whom have "deer" as part of their given names. It is said that antlers were originally the gift to the deer from Woman, and they remain the deer's link with the world of spirit. Antler is the material most suited to my work. It is the expression of transformation and rebirth. It is as natural to me as my name.

Yolai'kia Wapita'ska
White Deer Woman

Land Mother / Water Mother (Land Mother side)

Land Mother/Water Mother

It is from Land Mother and Water Mother, twin aspects of Grandmother Earth, that creatures learn those qualities known as instinct, salmon to swim upstream, geese to fly south for winter. None is forgotten; all are cared for.

(Water Mother side)

Father Sky/Mother Earth

Sky and Earth are the parents of the woodlands. Sky is the activating force of life, bringing heat and inspiration. Earth provides shelter and sustenance for her children.

Father Sky / Mother Earth (Mother Earth side)

(Father Sky side)

Mother of the Mountain

She stands at the top of Mount Lamentation in Quebec. Cradling her child, she gazes at the land of the Abenaki, confident that the Spirit will survive.

Mother of the Mountain

Bird/Shaman Transformation Amulet

Shaman bonds with his totem spirit, Raven, through his song and through the amethyst crystal, an energy bridge between worlds. Some ancients believed that when shamans passed from life their spirits remained in the form of crystals.

Owl Woman and Child Amulet

She has joined with Owl. She walks/flies between the physical and spirit worlds. Her bond is her power.

Bird/Shaman Transformation Amulet

Owl Woman and Child Amulet

Bear Evolution

The Abenaki regard Bear as their brother, as the "four-legged who walks two-legged."

Abenaki Mother and Child

May this child hold fast to the ways of his ancestors! May he learn to transform the old traditions into new life!

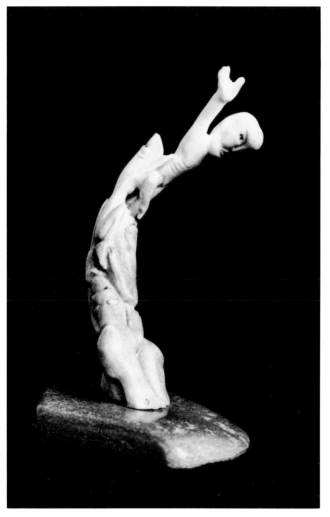

Bear Evolution

Abenaki Mother and Child

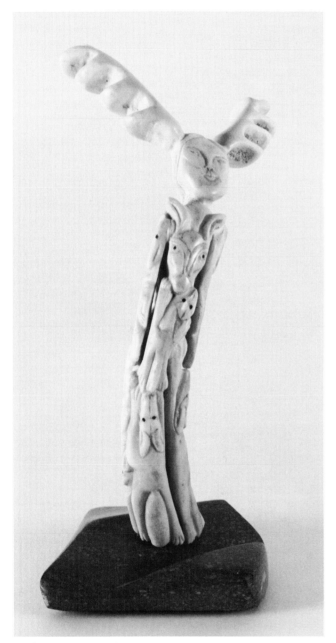

Red Deer Woman: Totem of the Wolves

Red Deer Woman, protector of deer, is mother love in her heart and spirit way in her antlers. Her body is Wolf, who helps keep the deer population strong. Reminding her of this balance, Wolf tugs on the braid which hangs down her back.

First Deer

The first deer on earth, unaware of danger, has yet to take his first step in a new world. His antlers, gift from Woman, are his connecting link to Spirit.

Red Deer Woman: Totem of the Wolves

First Deer

Wolf Clan Mother

Bonded to Wolf, she has given
birth to the first of the Wolf Clan.
Her child will learn to be a great
warrior. He will be sometimes wolf,
sometimes man, powerful in his
duality.

Wolf Clan Mother

Wolf Fetish

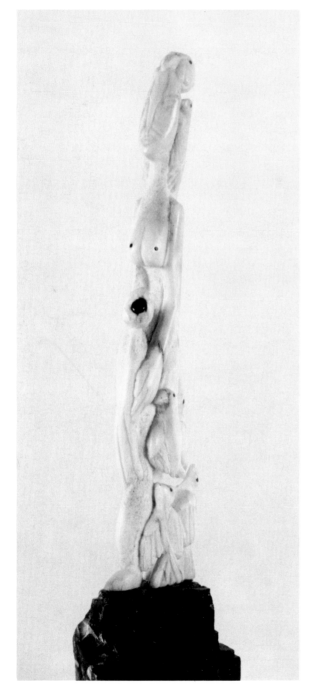

Sky Woman

Sky Woman

Sky Woman, a nighttime image, walks the heavens carrying in her hands a parcel of light, symbol of great events. She transports this ball of fire, this comet, through the darkness, while from her hair, birds tumble out into the dawn.

Shaman/Owl Transformation

Shaman is protected by his guardian, Great Horned Owl. His power comes from the union of his strength with that of his spirit companion.

Shaman/Owl Transformation